TOASTS

THE DIFFERENCE BETWEEN A GOOD NIGHT AND A GREAT NIGHT

WILLOW CREEK PRESS®

TOASTS

Published by Willow Creek Press, Inc.
P.O. Box 147, Minocqua, Wisconsin 54548

Printed in the United States

Table of Contents

To Health & Happiness

May we keep a little of the fuel of
youth to warm our body in old age.

Do not resist growing old—
many are denied the privilege.

May you live as long as you want,
may you never want as long as you live.

May the saddest day of your future be no
worse than the happiest day of your past.

May you live to be a hundred—
and decide the rest for yourself.

You're not as young as you used to be,
but you're not as old as you're
going to be—so watch it!

May you enter heaven late.

Good, better, best; Never let it rest.
Till your good is better,
and your better best.

Alcohol may be man's worst enemy, but the bible says love your enemy.

—Frank Sinatra

May your heart be light and happy,
May your smile be big and wide,
And may your pockets always have
a coin or two inside!

May we keep a little of the fuel of youth
to warm our body in old age.

A man is only as old as the woman he feels.

May the sunshine of comfort
dispel the clouds of despair.

To the most closely guarded secret
in this country—your real age.

Here's to your health! You make age curious,
time furious, and all of us envious.

Here's to you! No matter how old
you are, you don't look it!

To your good health, old friend, may you live for
a thousand years, and I be there to count them.

Everybody's
got to believe
in something.
I believe
I'll have
another beer.

—W. C. Fields

May you live to be a hundred years
with one extra year to repent.

To your health. May we drink one
together in ten years' time
and a few in between.

May you have the hindsight to know
where you've been, the foresight
to know where you are going,
and the insight to know when
you have gone too far.

May you live to be as old as your jokes.

May the frowns of misfortune
never rob innocence of its joy.

To middle age, when we begin to
exchange our emotions for symptoms.

Here's to a long life and a happy one.
A quick death and an easy one.
A good girl and an honest one.
A cold pint and another one.

May your life be as beautiful as a summer day
with just enough clouds to make
you appreciate the sunshine.

May you live to be a hundred—
and decide the rest for yourself.

May the clouds in your life be only
a background for a lovely sunset.

May misfortune follow you the rest of your life,
and never catch up.

Here's health to those I love,
and wealth to those who love me.

May you have been born on your
lucky star and may that star never
lose its twinkle.

Here's to health to my soul
and health to my heart;
Where this is going,
there's gone many a quart.

I drank to your health in company.
I drank to your health alone.
I drank to your health so many times,
I nearly ruined my own.

Here's a health to the future;
A sigh for the past;
We can love and remember,
And hope to the last.

May we never go to hell,
but always be on our way.

May time never turn your head gray.

May your troubles be less
and your blessings be more.
And nothing but happiness
come through your door.

May we look forward with happiness,
and backward without regret.

May we be happy and
our enemies know it.

In wine there
is wisdom, in
beer there is
freedom, in
water there
is bacteria.

—Benjamin Franklin

Here's to trusting your gut,
taking the occasional risk,
and never, ever looking back.

May we all meet on many more happy occasions.

Here's to a full belly,
a heavy purse,
and a light heart.

May your joys be as deep as the ocean,
and your misfortunes as light as its foam.

Here's to marriage, a feast where the grace
is sometimes better than the dinner.

May the single be married
and the married be happy.

May the warmth of our affections
survive the frosts of age.

Here's a health to your enemies' enemies!

I like whiskey. I always did, and that is why I never drink it.

—Robert E. Lee

Always remember to forget
the things that made you sad.
But never forget to remember
the things that made you glad.

May you be in heaven
fifteen minutes before the
devil knows you are dead.

Here's to eternity—
may we spend it in
as good company
as this night finds us.

To the old, long life and treasure;
To the young, all health and pleasure;
To the fair, their face,
With eternal grace;
And the rest, to be loved at leisure.

Happy birthday to you
And many to be,
With friends that are true
As you are to me!

Here's to eyes in your heads
and none in your spuds.

Another candle on your cake?
Well, that's no cause to pout,
Be glad that you have strength enough
To blow the damn thing out.

To wish you joy on your birthday
And all the whole year through,
For all the best that life can hold
Is none too good for you.

May you have the health of a salmon—
a strong heart and a wet mouth.

May you get all your wishes but one
so you always have something to strive for!

May you be poor in misfortune,
Rich in blessings,
Slow to make enemies,
And quick to make friends.
But rich or poor, quick or slow,
May you know nothing but happiness
From this day forward.

May we always have old wine,
old friends, and young cares.

To the Men & Women We Love

Here's to our sweethearts and our wives;
May our sweethearts soon become our wives.
And our wives ever remain our sweethearts.

Here's a toast to you,
And a toast to me,
And a toast to us both together;
And whatever we do,
And wherever we be,
May we always be birds of a feather.

Wine and women—
May we always have a taste for both.

May you live each day like your last,
and live each night like your first.

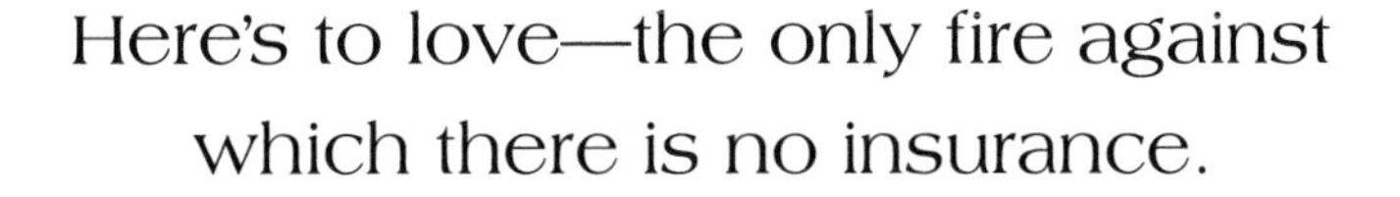

Here's to love—the only fire against
which there is no insurance.

To those who know me best and,
for some reason, still love me.

May the blossoms of love never be blighted,
And a true-hearted young woman
never be slighted.

Too much
of anything
is bad, but
too much
champagne
is just right.

—F. Scott Fitzgerald

Here's to a sweetheart,
a bottle, and a friend.
The first beautiful,
the second full,
the last ever faithful.

Here's to those who've
seen us at our best
and seen us at our worst
and can't tell the difference.

To moderation in all things—
except in love.

Here's to God's first thought, Man!
Here's to God's second thought, Woman!
Second thoughts are always best,
So here's to Woman!

Tis better to have loved and lost—
Than to marry and be bossed.

Here's to our wives and sweethearts—
And may they never meet.

A mocking eye,
A pair of lips
That's often why
A fellow trips.

Drink to fair woman, who, I think,
Is most entitled to it.
For if anything ever can drive me to drink,
She certainly could do it.

May your hands be forever clasped in friendship
And your hearts joined forever in love.

There's not a place on earth or heaven,
There's not a task to mankind given,
There's not a blessing or a woe,
There's not a whispered yes or no,
There's not a life or birth,
That has feather's weight of worth—
without a women in it.

Here's to those who'd love us
If only we cared.
Here's to those we'd love
If only we dared
To the life we love with those we love.

Here's to the girls of the American shore,
I love but one, I love no more;
Since she's not here to drink her part,
I drink her share with all my heart.

To the newlyweds:
May "for better or worse"
be far better than worse.

Here's to the husband
And here's to the wife;
May they remain
Lovers for life.

Here's to those who love us,
And here's to those who don't,
A smile for those who are willing to,
And a tear for those who won't.

To the ladies, God bless them,
May nothing distress them.

Let's drink to love,
which is nothing—
unless it's divided by two.

I know I'm drinking myself to a slow death, but then I'm in no hurry.

—Robert Benchley

Here's to you who halves my sorrows
and doubles my joys.

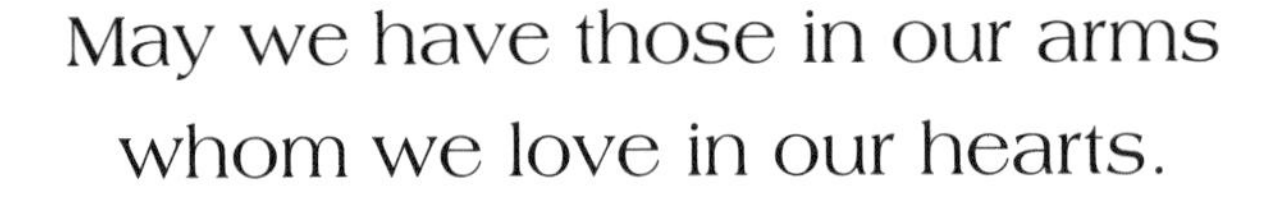

May we have those in our arms
whom we love in our hearts.

To the wings of love—
May they never lose a feather,
But soar up to the sky above,
And last and last forever.

To the sap in our family tree.

To our women, to our horses,
and the men who ride them.

A good wife and health
Are a man's best wealth.

May we have the unspeakable
good fortune to win a true heart,
and the merit to keep it.

Here's to love, liberty and
length of blissful days.

I drink to make other people more interesting.

—*Ernest Hemingway*

Here's to the prettiest,
Here's to the wittiest,
Here's to the truest of all who are true,
Here's to the neatest one,
Here's to the sweetest one,
Here's to them all in one—
here's to you.

May your love be as endless
as your wedding rings.

Here's to the heart that
fills as the bottle empties.

May we kiss those we please,
and please those we kiss.

Say it with flowers,
Say it with eats,
Say it with kisses,
Say it with sweets,
Say it with jewelry,
Say it with drink,
But always be careful
Not to say it with ink.

May we be loved by those we love.

I have known many,
liked a few,
Loved one—
Here's to you!

Drink to the girls and drink to their mothers,
Drink to the fathers and to their brothers;
Toast their dear healths as long as you're able,
And dream of their charms while under the table.

Here's to love.
It doesn't make the world go 'round,
It's what makes the ride worthwhile.

To life: The first half is
ruined by our parents
and the second half
by our children.

Because I love you truly,
Because you love me, too,
My very greatest happiness
Is sharing life with you.

Here's to lovers everywhere—
the have-beens, the are-nows,
and the may-bes.

To Friends Near & Far

There are good ships,
and there are wood ships,
The ships that sail the sea.
But the best ships, are friendships,
And may they always be.

Our little group has always been,
and always will until the end.

To our best friends,
who know the worst about us
but refuse to believe it.

Our enemies never drink,
Our friends always do,
So let's drink this drink,
And tell between the two.

May the roof above us never fall in,
and may we friends gathered
below never fall out.

Here's to our friends—
in the hopes that they,
wherever they are,
are drinking to us.

I may be drunk, Miss, but in the morning I will be sober and you will still be ugly.

—Winston Churchill

Friends forever,
enemies never,
may we cut through the bullshit,
always together.

May our friendship never fail,
May we always be kind,
I'll post your bail,
If you post mine.

To friendships and to drinking and
to friendships forged by drinking.

Nothing but the best for our hostess.
That's why she has us as friends.

You are only as strong as
the tables you dance on,
the drinks you mix
and the friends you roll with.

Here's to you and here's to me,
Friends may we always be!
But, if by chance we disagree,
Up yours! Here's to me!

Candy is dandy, but liquor is quicker.

—Ogden Nash

Here's to the nights we'll never
remember with the friends
we'll never forget.

Here's to you, here's to me.
Here's to snapchats
no one else shall see.

Good company, good wine,
good welcome can make good people.

May we all be blessed with love from one,
friendship from many and goodwill from all.

I keep my friends close,
but my enemies closer.

Friendship's the wine of life.
Let's drink of it and to it.

Here's to those who wish us well,
and those who don't can go to hell.

May our house always be too
small to hold all our friends.

To goodbyes—
that they never be spoken.
To friendships—
may they never be broken.

May we always part with regret
and meet again with pleasure.

May the hinges of our friendship never grow rusty.

Strike hands with me.
The glass is brim.
The dew is on the heather.
And love is good, and life is long,
and friends are best together.

A little health, a little wealth,
A little house and freedom:
With some few friends for certain ends
But little cause to need 'em.

May the friends of our youth
be the companions of our old age.

It is around the table that
friends understand best
the warmth of being together.

A toast to our host
And a song from the short and tall of us,
May he live to be
The guest of all of us!

Happy are we met, happy have we been,
Happy may we part, and happy we meet again.

Here's to our hostess,
considerate and sweet;
Her wit is endless,
but when do we eat?

Here's to a friend. He knows you well
and likes you just the same.

The pain of parting is nothing
to the joy of meeting again.

Alcohol gives you infinite patience for stupidity.

—Sammy Davis, Jr.

May your right hand always
Be stretched out in friendship
And never in want.

Here's to a fellow who smiles
When life runs along like a song.
And here's to the lad who can smile
When everything goes dead wrong.

Here's to our friendship;
May it be reckoned long as a lifetime,
Close as a second.

Old friends are scarce,
New friends are few;
Here's hoping I've found
One of each in you.

May your tobacco never run out,
your library never turn musty,
your cellar never go dry,
and your friends never turn foes.

A day for toil, an hour for sport,
But for a friend life is too short.

To the Poets & Philosophers

In days of old the night-cap
Was worn outside the head:
Let's put ours in the inside
And then—let's go to bed.

May your well never run dry.

May we be like mighty oaks,
which, after all, are only acorns
that held their ground.

Here's to blue skies and green lights.

May you live to learn well,
and learn to live well.

May you have warm words
on a cold evening,
A full moon on a dark night,
And the road downhill all
the way to your door.

May you dance as if no one were watching,
Sing as if no one were listening,
And live every day as if it were your last.

To lying, stealing, cheating and drinking.
If you're going to lie, lie for a friend.
If you're going to steal, steal a heart.
If your going to cheat, cheat death.
And if you're going to drink, drink with me.

May our pleasures be free
from the stings of remorse.

And fill them high with generous juice,
As generous as your mind,
And pledge me in this generous toast—
The whole of human kind!

May he who thinks to cheat another,
cheat himself the most.

May the strength of
three be in your journey.

May we never murmur without cause,
and never have cause to murmur.

Rejoice, and be of good cheer!
For THEY are out there,
and WE are in here!

Here's to alcohol, the rose colored glasses of life.

—F. Scott Fitzgerald

May the sunshine of comfort
dispel the clouds of despair.

May we always be wise
enough to follow the wiser.

Here's to the fellow who smiles,
When life rolls along like a song,
And here's to the chap who can smile,
When everything goes dead wrong.

To long lives and short wars.

May we never let our tongues cut our throat
nor quarrel with our bread and butter.

When going up the hill of prosperity,
May you never meet any friend coming down.

May the tide of fortune float us
into the harbor of content.

It is best to rise from life
as from the banquet,
neither thirsty nor drunken.

When I read about the evils of drinking, I gave up reading.

—*Henny Youngman*

May your shadow never grow less.

May we be known by our deeds,
not by our mortgages.

May the winds of fortune sail you,
May you sail a gentle sea.
May it always be the other guy
who says, 'this drink's on me.

May your luck ever spread,
like jelly on bread.

May your heart be light and happy,
May your smile be big and wide,
And may your pockets always
have a coin or two inside!

May your fire be as warm
as the weather is cold.

May you always distinguish
between the weeds and the flowers.

May the ships at sea never be bottoms up.

It matters not if the wine glass
is half empty or half full,
clearly there's room for more!

Here's to it, down to it,
damn the man that can't do it,
shovel it over to me cause I'm used to it!

Here's to the man who is wisest and best,
Here's to the man who with judgment is blest,
Here's to the man who's as smart as can be—
I drink to the man who agrees with me!

Drink until the sun comes up,
Drink until the sun goes down,
If you drink on both occasions
You will never wear a frown.

May you always have a clean shirt,
a clear conscience,
and enough coins in your
pocket to buy a pint.

No wasps near your honey,
but bees in your hive.

May the road rise to meet you.
May the wind be always at your back.

Here's to the good old days,
They were better days I vow;
You could buy a whole hen then
For what an egg costs now.

May we never flatter our
superiors or insult our inferiors.

May the rocks in your field turn to gold.

Here's to you and here's to me,
Wherever we may roam;
And here's to the health and happiness
Of the ones who are left at home.

A speedy calm to the storms of life.

May we love peace enough to fight for it.

May you live as long as you like,
And have what you like as long as you live.

May your neighbors respect you,
trouble neglect you,
the angels protect you,
and heaven accept you.

May all the giant hearts be tall as day,
may all your winter nights be warm as May.

We lit the candle from both ends,
it wouldn't last the night,
but ah my fellows and my friends,
the flame it burned so bright.

Be at war with your vices,
at peace with your neighbors,
and let every new year
find you a better man.

Some take their gold in minted mold,
And some in harps hereafter;
But give me mine in tresses fine,
And keep the change--in laughter.

Within this goblet, rich and deep,
I cradle all my woes to sleep.

I don't have a drinking problem 'cept when I can't get a drink.

—Tom Waits

May you have the hindsight
to know where you've been,
the foresight to know
where you're going,
and the insight to know
when you're going too far.

Here's to the wisdom of all
who come to us for advice.

Take everything in moderation—
including moderation.

I've traveled many a highway
I've walked for many a mile.
Here's to the people who made my day
To the people who waved and smiled.

None so deaf as those who will not hear.
None so blind as those who will not see.
But I'll wager none so deaf nor so blind that he
Sees not nor hears me say come drink this beer.

May our wants be sown in so fruitful
a soil as to produce immediate relief.

While we live, let us live.

Cheerfulness, content, and competency.
Cheerfulness in our cups,
Content in our minds,
Competency in our pockets.

May the works of our nights
never fear the daylight.

So live that when you come to die,
even the undertaker will feel sorry for you.

May our faults be written
on the seashore, and every
good action prove a
wave to wash them out.

To the riotous enjoyment
of a quiet conscience.

May the grass grow long on
the road to hell for want of use.

May the Devil say a prayer for you.

The worst
thing about
some men is
that when
they are not
drunk they
are sober.

—William Butler Yeats

To Food & Drink

Now don't say you can't swear off drinking; it's easy. I've done it a thousand times.

—*W. C. Fields*

Here's to bourbon friends knowing
things that beer friends don't.

To wine. It improves with age—
I like it more the older I get.

Here's to us, my good, fat friends,
To bless the things we eat;
For it has been full many a year,
Since we have seen our feet.

Cheers, cheers, now bring more beers.

May your coffee and slanders against you
be ever alike—without grounds.

In heaven there is no beer—
That's why we drink ours here.

To friendship and joy,
to all our good times.
Here's to many great things,
but mostly to wine.

Here's to the good time I must have had!

To us, to this night,
to love and good cheer!
To thinking we're so clever,
when that's just the beer.

Lift 'em high and drain 'em dry.
To the guy who says, "My turn to buy!"

Here's to doing and drinking,
not sitting and thinking.

Let no man thirst for lack of real ale.

If wine tells truth, and so have said the wise;
It makes me laugh to think how brandy lies.

My friends are the best friends
Loyal, willing and able.
Now let's get to drinking!
All glasses off the table!

Then a smile, and a glass,
and a toast and a cheer,
For all the good wine,
and we've some of it here.

May you always have love in your
hearts and beer in your belly.

When wine enlivens the heart
May friendship surround the table.

A warm toast.
Good company.
A fine wine.
May you enjoy all three.

Here's to clean glasses and old corks.

As we ride over the bad roads of life,
may good wine be our spur.

In victory, you deserve champagne,
in defeat, you need it.

Then once again, before we part,
My empty glass shall ring;
And he that has the warmest heart
Shall loudest laugh and sing.

To the thirst that is yet to come.

Alcohol is like love. The first kiss is magic, the second is intimate, the third is routine. After that you take the girl's clothes off.

—Raymond Chandler

Pain makes you stronger.
Tears make you braver.
Heartbreak makes you wiser.
And vodka makes you not
remember any of that crap.

A bumper of good liquor
Will end a contest quicker
Than justice, judge or vicar;
So fill a cheerful glass,
And let good humor pass.

Of all my favorite things to do,
The utmost is to have a brew.
My love grows for my foamy friend,
With each thirst-quenching elbow bend.
Beer's so frothy, smooth and cold;
It's paradise, pure liquid gold.
Yes, beer means many things to me.
That's all for now, I gotta pee.

Tis hard to tell which is best,
music, food, drink, or rest.

May we never be out of spirits.

Drink because you are happy, but never because you are miserable.

—G. K. Chesterton

Here's to steak when you're hungry,
Whiskey when you're dry,
A lover when you need one,
And Heaven when you die.

You're a gentleman and a scholar and a good judge of bad liquor.

For every wound, a balm.
For every sorrow, cheer.
For every storm, a calm.
For every thirst, a beer.

Here's to whiskey, scotch and rye,
Amber, smooth, and clear,
Not as sweet as a woman's lips,
But a damn sight more sincere.

Show me a nation whose national
beverage is beer, and I'll show you
an advanced toilet technology.

Never drink anything without first smelling it,
Never sign anything without first reading it.
Never dive into pools of depth unknown,
And rarely drink—if you are alone.

To alcohol—a liquid good for preserving
almost anything except secrets.

Let us make our glasses kiss;
Let us quench the sorrow-cinders.

I love to drink martinis.
Two at the very most.
Three I'm under the table.
Four I'm under the host!

Here's to old wine and young women.

Let's drink the liquid of amber so bright;
Let's drink the liquid with foam snowy white;
Let's drink the liquid that brings all good cheer;
Oh, where is the drink like old-fashioned beer?

Let us have wine and women, mirth and laughter,
Sermons and soda-water the day after.

Stir the eggnog, lift the toddy,
Happy New Year, everybody.

God made man
As frail as a bubble,
God made love,
And love made trouble,
God made wine,
And is it any sin
For man to drink wine
To drown trouble in?

Grasp the bowl; in nectar sinking
Man of sorrow, drown thy thinking!

Here's to a "dram" and a good long one.

Good pies and strong beer.

To Moms cooking:
May my wife never find out
how bad it really was.

Ale's a strong wrestler,
Flings all it hath met;
And makes the ground slippery,
Though it not be wet.

I am drinking ale today.

Let us be lazy
in everything,
except in
loving and
drinking,
except in
being lazy.

—Gotthold Ephraim Lessing

To the Funny & Clever

May all your ups and downs
be between the sheets.

Another day another bender.
No retreat, no surrender.

May our sons have rich fathers
and beautiful mothers.

May your wit be quick and your game be slick,
and may you never be tagged in an unflattering pic.

Here's to being the story other people tell.

May we get what we want,
but never what we deserve.

Here's to snatching kisses and the other way around.

Here's to the ships of our navy,
Here's to the ladies of our land,
May the former be well-rigged,
And the latter be well-manned.

On the chest of a barmaid in Sale
Were tattooed the prices of ale.
And on her behind,
For the sake of the blind,
Was the same information in Braille!

May thy life be long and happy,
Thy cares and sorrows few;
And the many friends around thee
Prove faithful, fond and true.

Here's to staying positive and testing negative.

To all of us here, so smart and so fine,
and to whomever's tab this is on,
because it sure as Hell ain't on mine.

Here's to you. You may not be as wise
as an owl, but you're always a hoot.

Here's to the top,
Here's to the middle,
Here's hoping we all get a little.

Here's to making some new accomplices.

Here's to alcohol: the cause of, and answer to, all of life's problems.

—Matt Groening

May your bank account always
be bigger than your troubles.

Here's to the roses and lilies in bloom,
You in my arms and I in your room.
A door that is locked, a key that is lost,
A bird, and a bottle, and a bed badly tossed,
and a night that is fifty years long.

Here's to being single, drinking doubles, and seeing triple!

May we be who our dogs think we are.

May those that love us, love us;
and those that don't love us,
may God turn their hearts;
if he can't turn there hearts,
then may he turn their ankles,
so we'll know them by their limp.

As you slide down
the banister of life,
may the splinters never
point the wrong way.

To the holidays— all 365 of them.

Alcohol is necessary for a man so that he can have a good opinion of himself, undisturbed be the facts.

—Finley Peter Dunne

Here's to it,
And from it,
And to it again,
'Cause we might not
be here to do it again.

To my schizophrenic friend.
He's good people.

To your genitalia:
May they never fail ya, or jail ya.

Drink today and drown all sorrow,
You may perhaps not be here tomorrow,
Best while you have it, use your breath,
There is no drinking after death.

Here's to the heat. Not the heat that
brings down barns and shanties,
but the heat that brings down
bras and panties.

Here's to lobster tail and beer.
Three of my favorite things.

I used to know a clever toast,
But now I cannot think of it.
So fill your glass to anything,
And bless your souls, I'll drink it!

Life is a waste of time,
and time is a waste of life.
So let's get wasted all of the time,
and have the time of our life.

Better to be a well-known drunkard
than an anonymous alcoholic.

When we drink, we get drunk.
When we get drunk, we fall asleep.
When we fall asleep, we commit no sin.
When we commit no sin, we go to heaven.
So let's all get drunk and go to heaven.

To hell: May the stay there
be as fun as the way there.

Here's to the stories you'll tell, and
the secrets you'll want to keep.

Here's to the lasses we've loved, my lad,
Here's to the lips we've pressed;
For of kisses and lasses,
Like liquor in glasses,
The last is always the best.

Steady your glasses,
Here comes the gale,
Batten down the hatches,
And lean well over the rail.

We're only here for a short time,
let's make it a good time!

Here's to a guy who is never blue,
Here's to a buddy who is ever true,
Here's to a pal, no matter what the load,
Never declines one for the road.

With this glass, rich and deep
We cradle all our sorrows to sleep.

Let us drink with impunity
Or anyone else who's buying.

Good luck till we are tired of it.

The worse you are at thinking, the better you are at drinking.

—Terry Goodkind

Let us drink to bread,
for without bread,
there would be no toast.

Over the teeth, over the gums,
look out stomach here it comes.

We drink to your coffin.
May it be built from the wood
of a hundred-year-old oak tree
that I shall plant tomorrow.

To my partner in crime,
full of beauty and wit,
may we have so much fun,
before this night turns to shit.

Here's to the guys who's love us,
the losers who's lost us,
and the lucky bastards
that get to meet us.

May you sleep like a log,
but not like a sawmill.

Always do sober what you said you'd do drunk. That will teach you to keep your mouth shut.

—Ernest Hemingway

Here's to all the poor people
Because without them
we'd never look rich.

To alcohol—
The cause and the solution
to all the world's problems.

Here's to your nose,
here's to your chin,
here's to the hole,
in-between it goes in!

Always remember to forget
The troubles that passed away.
But never forget to remember
The blessings that come each day.

May the face of every good news
and the back of every bad
news be towards us.

A toast to the wise
And a toast to the foollish,
A toast to your eyes—
May they never grow mulish!

Here's to the heights of heaven,
Here's to the depths of hell,
Here's to the girl who can have a good time
And has sense enough not to tell.

Here's to modesty,
beauty's best companion.

May the thorns of life only serve
to give a zest to its flowers.

May we never do worse!